I0390923

Online Marketing

'50 useful online blog articles to get you on your way.'

www.blogbyte.co.uk

© Copyright 2013 Blog Byte

Contents

Blog 1	How important is a company logo?	Page 4 - 5
Blog 2	Branding	Page 6 - 7
Blog 3	Facebook, what's it all about?	Page 7 - 8
Blog 4	Social networking - business or pleasure?	Page 9 - 10
Blog 5	The key to effective marketing	Page 11 - 12
Blog 6	What is, and how do I blog?	Page 12 - 14
Blog 7	Email Marketing Tips	Page 14 - 16
Blog 8	Twitter, what's it all about?	Page 16 - 17
Blog 9	Does link building work?	Page 17 - 18
Blog 10	Email marketing or SPAM?	Page 19 - 20
Blog 11	Objectives and toolkits	Page 21 - 22
Blog 12	Making call to actions work	Page 22 - 24
Blog 13	Ways to build loyalty online	Page 24 - 26
Blog 14	Using Royalty Free Image Stock	Page 26 - 27
Blog 15	Online Vs Offline Networking	Page 27 - 29
Blog 16	Why Should I use Linked-In	Page 29 - 30
Blog 17	Tips for surviving a recession	Page 30 - 32
Blog 18	Top Website Design Tips - Part 1	Page 32 - 34
Blog 19	Top Website Design Tips - Part 2	Page 34 - 36
Blog 20	Do people feel safe buying online?	Page 36 - 37
Blog 21	How to take the perfect picture	Page 38 - 39
Blog 22	How to make your site easy to view	Page 39 - 40
Blog 23	The key to effective web optimisation	Page 41 - 43
Blog 24	When is a good time to rebrand?	Page 43 - 44
Blog 25	What is Expeditionary Marketing?	Page 45 - 46

Contents

Blog 26	Colourful branding for a colourful company!	Page 47 - 48
Blog 27	Top 5 social networking websites	Page 48 - 49
Blog 28	How has Marketing changed over 10 years?	Page 50 - 51
Blog 29	How important is a company website?	Page 51 - 53
Blog 30	How often should I be sending my e-shots?	Page 53 - 54
Blog 31	How to approach business like an entrepreneur	Page 54 - 57
Blog 32	Marketing to a local audience	Page 57 - 59
Blog 33	The Importance of Website Imagery	Page 59 - 60
Blog 34	Twitter - I'm set up, now what?	Page 60 - 62
Blog 35	Why are my customers not buying?	Page 63 - 64
Blog 36	Top tips for Social Media engagement	Page 64 - 66
Blog 37	Website design - Where do I start?	Page 66 - 68
Blog 38	What does a marketing plan involve?!	Page 68 - 71
Blog 39	What is the shelf life of a company website?	Page 71 - 72
Blog 40	Dangers of social networking	Page 72 - 74
Blog 41	How to collect an email base	Page 74 - 75
Blog 42	What are royalty free images?	Page 76 - 77
Blog 43	What should an e-shot include?	Page 77 - 78
Blog 44	Words of warning - email marketing	Page 79 - 80
Blog 45	What social media icons should I include?	Page 80 - 81
Blog 46	Top 3 upcoming social media sites	Page 81 - 82
Blog 47	How do people know you have a website?	Page 82 - 83
Blog 48	How does Apple market so effectively?	Page 84 - 85
Blog 49	Where do businesses miss a marketing trick?	Page 86 - 87
Blog 50	Top 5 functions every website should have	Page 88 - 89

Blog 1
How important is a company logo?

A company logo is the face of the business; it is an effective way to give a company a personal image that people can connect with, no matter what the size of the organisation. It has to be unique and memorable whilst reflecting values of the business.

It is extremely important for companies to have a well executed integrated marketing campaign to ensure consistency of message and use media channels to their full potential. A good company logo can act as the lynch pin for this. Consumers will get used to seeing the logo and know instantly who the company is and what they are about.

A good logo acts as a silent salesman, it allows instant brand recognition from consumers and it can conjure emotions and thought processes connected with the brand. A consumer is more likely to choose a company with a logo they recognise because of the connections they have associated with it – Looking at it simply people are more likely to trust a person who they recognise.

Two elements have to be carefully considered when designing a logo:

Firstly design – this can either be simple or complex, this decision depends completely on the brand image. It is also important to be sure that the logo is still effective when reproduced. If a logo is too complex when printed on a small scale it may lose its effectiveness.

Secondly colour – different colours bring with them varying connotations. Banks tend to use gold, green and blue to project a mature and trustworthy image whereas fast food restaurants and companies aimed mainly at the children's market chose bright colours such as yellow and red. There are also differences with the meaning of colours in different countries so if you're dealing with a global brand this might be something to take into consideration.

Taking the Chanel logo as an example; the use of black and white projects an elegant and classic image in keeping with that of the brand. The backward C's further this. If you were to ask any fashion conscious male or female they are guaranteed to know the Chanel logo – I would even go so far as to say that many people who aren't interested in fashion would know it too.

This is also evidence that some products would be nothing without their logos. Imagine most designer bags minus a logo, many of them would just be simple bags and they wouldn't cost half their current price.

Another way to grab consumer's attention is to have hidden meanings within logos this can cause discussion around the brand. However it is a good idea not to make them too metaphorical otherwise people may miss the point

So how important is a company logo? Very. A logo is so important that companies are attempting to sue others who they believe to be copying them. An example of this is back in 2008 Lacoste attempted to stop a Gloucestershire dentist from using a crocodile as the logo for the business.

A logo is a brilliant opportunity to connect with the consumer and cement your business into their brand repertoire. Don't miss out...

Blog 2
Branding

- Branding is your brand name
- Branding is your company logo
- Branding is the people who work for you.

The list is endless and is more comprehensive than initially thought......

Every company has a name, employees and possibly a logo but these alone don't make them brands.

Brands are of course influenced by the efforts made by the company to project a certain image to customers through advertising, marketing and PR. However the second half of branding is based on the thoughts and feelings that people associate with the products/ service. If companies can identify these cognitive and affective processes then they will be able to target their customers more effectively and even influence these processes.

Does a good brand bring any benefits?

Creating successful branding for your business can be crucial, especially in hard financial times such as the recent recession.

Having a successful brand provokes loyalty from your customers as they feel a connection with your company and would prefer to continue giving their custom.

Branding makes you memorable in amongst an already crowded market place. Customers can sometimes feel a sense of 'information overload' when they enter the market place, a known logo along with an integrated marketing campaign can act as a safety net as they search for something familiar.

Customers associate slick brands with successful and professional businesses. Are you projecting the right image? Your business must have strengths, that is why it succeeds so tell your customers about them.

Branding your product or service is not easy but for this precise reason it is something that is worth doing. By investing both money and time into your brand now you should reap rewards in the future as customers remain loyal to the brand that they know and love. Why not differentiate your brand from others by putting in extra effort to give yours the edge?

Blog 3
Facebook, what's it all about?

It all began in Mark Zuckerberg's Harvard University student room back in 2004 and has been transformed into one of the largest social networking sites online with over 600 million active users. Facebook can be explained as a social networking site designed for individuals who want to easily stay in touch with friends, family and co-workers.

Users are able to add friends either by email address or search for them by name. They can then request their friendship, share photos, update their status and write on their wall. It is essentially like texting but on the internet, however it is important to note that others can see it unless it is sent by private message.

Facebook has played a part in being responsible for the changes in the way people interact. Users are able to keep in touch with friends who have moved to the other side of the world, see their pictures and speak to them on Facebook chat – an IM service at the bottom of your webpage which allows you to see when other users are online. However Facebook has been at the centre of a long running debate about how the younger generation are not taking part in 'real' conversations and prefer to 'poke' each other over an internet site.

It is not just individuals who can benefit from the site, it is also a helpful tool for businesses. Companies can create groups and pages with information about themselves and their products. Facebook users can then decide to 'Become a Fan' or join a group to offer their support. There have been a few occasions where Facebook groups have had an impact on wider society, for example the 2009 Christmas number 1 was Rage Against The Machine instead of X-factor winner Joe McElderry.

Geo-location tagging company Foursquare is now facing competition from Facebook who have just launched 'Facebook Places' - a new application for mobile phones to allow users to alert friends in real time where they are, what they are doing and who they are with. For now it is only available in the US however Facebook have said it will be rolled out to other countries within the next few months. This application will no doubt reignite the debate of online privacy and whether the 'youths of today' are sharing too much information. Facebook stress that users chose to opt into the application and decide whether or not to check-in at a certain location.

Privacy settings on Facebook are easy to change and it is suggested that individuals make sure that they are au fait with just what others can see.

The best way to learn about something is to experience it so set up your Facebook account today!

A fantastic guide to anyone with no idea about Facebook who wants to start: http://news.cnet.com/newbies-guide-to-facebook/

Blog 4
Social networking - business or pleasure?

Social networking has exploded onto the scene in recent years and I believe its arrival has changed the way in which people communicate forever. I was born straight into the technological era and had my first mobile phone at the age of 8 – although I had no idea what to do with it and can't remember using it....

Mobile phones with their ability to text, access the internet and emails have made social networking a way of life. I think nothing of messaging a friend on Facebook and if I don't receive an email notifying me that someone has commented on my status or written on my wall all day I'm slightly offended.

Luckily I am of the generation that I can take full advantage of these technological advancements. Facebook has always been there, Twitter and LinkedIn, all of these sites have me as a member and I use each of them actively for what I deem to be their role.

It wasn't until I took my first step into the grown up working world I realised that it might not be a good idea to add everyone I know onto Facebook. Would my new boss really want to see what I was doing outside of work? I have to admit, I'm not much of a rebel and only tend to go out once or twice a week but is it appropriate for them to know who my friends are, where I am and what I'm planning on doing?

There are many dangers associated with having colleagues and bosses on Facebook: There have been a number of stories in the news about employees being taken to court because of writing derogatory status's about their work and in some cases their fellow employees. (http://www.news24.com/SouthAfrica/News/Fired-over-Facebook-20090527) There are unwritten 'rules' regarding using peoples pictures for business reasons – they are a minefield and depend completely on the person in question. There also seems to be no set regulations on using information that they might publish. For example if you are friends with a colleague who is under performing and you see their status updates about relationship problems should you alter the way you deal with the situation?

With one fifth of employees spending more than 45 hours a week at work(http://www.cipd.co.uk/subjects/hrpract/hoursandholidays/working-hours-time-off.htm) their choice of who they spend their time with is limited. The likelihood is that they see their workmates more often than their friends.

This in fact begs the question: Are the lines between individuals work lives and private lives becoming blurred? And do they now overlap?

The emergence of LinkedIn.com seemed to fill this niche. When asked what it is I reply: 'It's just like Facebook but for my work people'. A very technical explanation, but accurate.

Working in PR I know that building relationships is the basis of my career. LinkedIn provides me with a platform to do this, however it keeps it professional as there is very little personal information about me there apart from my previous work, one profile picture and status updates are more likely to be interesting links rather than how I am feeling.

Let's call it clear cut: Facebook for friends and LinkedIn for business colleagues. What happens if your boss requests your friendship on Facebook to tag you in pictures of the Christmas party or invites you to join the company group. You can't exactly reject. Or can you? It all depends on the type of business that you work for, each individual has to decide how much information they allow to be online and who they want to access it.

In conclusion social networking can be used for both professional and personal reasons. However there are different sites for different applications and care should be taken to make sure that the two don't overlap.... not too much anyway.

Blog 5
The Key to Effective Marketing

It would be easy to give just one element of the marketing plan and claim that it was the 'key' to effective marketing. It could be getting the right message, understanding your target audience or making sure you evaluate the campaign properly. But it's not...

Consumers sometimes fail to differentiate between marketing strategies from different companies, getting confused by mixed messages. This highlights the need to have an integrated campaign. This task has been made harder by the introduction of new methods brought by the internet.

A successful marketing campaign will utilise both online and offline methods together in a partnership to use them to their full potential. If companies just concentrate on offline methods it could be said they are not moving with the times or keeping up with their target market. Online methods such as e-newsletter, article marketing, having a presence on twitter and social networking sites can either strengthen relationships with consumers by encouraging them into two-way communications or bombard them if not used correctly.

When thinking of a marketing plan the following questions should be asked:

Situational analysis – Where is your business now?
Objectives – Where do you want it to be?

Public - Who are you trying to target?

Message - What are you saying to them?

Methods - How are you planning on telling them?

Timescale - When are you going to tell them by?

Budget - How much will it cost you to tell them?

Evaluation and review - Have you told them effectively and do they now know what you wanted them to?

It is extremely useful to set objectives at the beginning of the campaign as they can be used as a benchmark for measurements and also as a constant reminder of where you want the business to be.

If all the above questions are thought about in turn and implemented together in a well thought out, cohesive and integrated campaign, it is highly likely that your marketing will be effective.

In reality the key to an effective campaign isn't one thing it is making sure that all the elements work together.

Blog 6
What is, and how do I blog?

For many people the word blog means very little. Often when talking to people about my blog the answer is: 'oh I don't know about anything like that!'

However they are not reserved for the elite. Indeed setting one up is easier than a lot of people think. Everyone with something to say and an internet connection can have one.

The beauty of blogs is that they can be used for a variety of reasons. They are an effective way to encourage discussion and engage an audience with a topic, product and organisation. This interaction with consumers can benefit an organisation as you can gain invaluable feedback straight from the direct users of you business. People are likely to leave feedback and comments online because it is easy to do so, gone are the days when you had to write a letter to head office regarding the service.

There are many different platforms upon which you can set up your blog. In my experience Wordpress and Blogger are the most popular and the easiest to set up, however many others exist such as: dotemplate, Weebly, Templatr, psycho and Firdamatic. It is important to find one that works for you. You can personalise your blog by choosing different themes to suit the personality of your blog and by adding widgets such as a live twitter link.

Blogs can be promoted using other social media tools such as Facebook, Twitter and search engines like Google. However they can also be done by more traditional methods such as word of mouth. Unfortunately, the content can be the best, your ideas original, the layout perfect, but there is the risk that people might not see it, so it is a good idea to continue promoting your blog to gain more views and followers.

There has been a rise in the popularity of guest blogging – this is when an individual who maybe has their own blog, writes a post for yours or vice-versa. This is a brilliant way of sharing traffic as all the followers from their website, if they like your post, are likely to look on your website.

Overall, blogging is great and slightly addictive, so why not get writing!

Our top 5 tips for blogging:
1. **Make it interesting**
2. **Add pictures to break up the text**
3. **Follow other bloggers**

4. Don't make your posts too long if possible, people tend to zone out online
5. And most importantly – Don't forget to spell check!

Blog 7
Email Marketing Tips

Sending a well designed and targeted Email can complement any Marketing strategy and will ensure that your customers receive relevant information that will improve your brand awareness and potentially revenue.

Email Shots have become a more accepted part of Marketing and are now used by many businesses, as opposed to SPAM which are untargeted, invaluable and irrelevant Emails - also see our blog on: Email Marketing or SPAM

If you are intending to send an Email to your client base here are several top tips to ensure that you get results:

Target your Audience

Ensure that your audience is relevant and targeted, this will not only make sure that your Email is read by a larger proportion of the recipients but fewer clients are likely to unsubscribe and will continue to want to receive your e-shots. If you have your own database of existing customers that you can use then this will ensure that your audience is as targeted as it can be. Be very careful about obtaining random databases of customers as these are likely to be totally useless unless they are purchased from a reputable company.

Make your Call to Action Clear

What do you want from your targeted customers or clients? Make sure whether you want them to call you, Email you, buy now, subscribe, write to or join, ensure that it is clear, concise and well placed on the Email. If necessary repeat it, but make sure it stands out and is prominent on the page.

Company Brand

Ensure that your Email Marketing reflects your existing company brand too, so that your client's are already familiar with the look and feel. This not only subliminally links your brand together but will put existing customers at ease with the Email and ensure they do not think it is SPAM and in turn deleting it.

Succinct and explanatory content

Ensure that your content is succinct and explanatory, you do not need to be too wordy with Email shots, as recipients will often not be willing to read pages and pages of text (this obviously depends on how specific your Email client base is).

Emphasised words

Emphasise your words and text, stylise headings and sub headings, make your Email exciting to read by breaking the text up with good use of font style and weight. Also use sporadic imagery to break the text up, but the key, is good placement of your text and the messages that they give in a way that is easy on the eye and making important words stand out.

Check Spelling and Punctuation

Punctuation you would have thought is not even worth mentioning, well you'd be wrong! You have spent weeks getting the content together for your Email Marketing, you have canvassed your staff for great and exciting stories to include and you have a raft of imagery that will really catch the eye, you have compiled it all and it is looking absolutely fantastic.. Send, send, send - right? Wrong. Check spelling and punctuation before sending. This is very important and often overlooked.

Track, Analyse and Act on Results

You have sent your exciting, interesting, well worded targeted Email, so that's it - great job! Hold on, not quite.. You will need to track the progress of your Email if you are to understand exactly what is going on with regards to your recipients reading, opening, forwarding or acting upon your Email. If you have compiled a well targeted Email you want to ensure that your readers are getting the most from it, also you want to be able to see where are what recipients are interested in so you can follow up with them and in turn generate opportunities and leads. By using an effective tracking and analysing tool you can then improve your next email based on the stats you have collected.

Blog 8
Twitter, what's it all about?

What have I got in common with M C Hammer and Duncan Bannatyne? We are all slightly obsessed with posting 140 character messages to our followers at least once a day...

Just over 4 years ago, Twitter was launched. Defined as a free micro-blogging service that allows people to read and send messages, called tweets, Twitter has certainly made its mark.

Once you have signed up to Twitter you can build up followers who search for you using your user name or find you on one of the profiles they follow. Tweeters can post links, pictures and status updates whenever they want. Mobile phone providers have created applications that can be downloaded so people can tweet on the go, users can also tweet by SMS.

Back in 1876 the telephone was invented, people were able to talk to others as much as they liked for as long as they liked but now society has changed. Twitter has revolutionised methods of communication. It suits the business person of 2013, who truly believes there are not enough hours in the day. They can keep up with friends, business colleagues, competitors, job offers and news headlines easily.

Twitter puts the emphasis back on the individual, they choose how often they use it, what they use it for and how many people they follow. By offering this tailored service Twitter is whatever the users make of it – the more you put in, the more you get out.

Businesses are also taking advantage of the Twitter Bug that has hit the World. With 75 million users, businesses that overlook the importance of Twitter and don't include it in their marketing plan are missing out. The service allows companies to connect with their target audience like never before. They can share information, monitor customer trends and gain feedback effectively and in real time.

As far as 'jumping on the bandwagon' goes, this is definitely one to get on!

Blog 9
Does link building work?

Links to and from your website have been the foundations upon which search engines have identified and ranked the popularity of all websites for years. The idea being that links count as 'votes' for your site.

It should be a combination of quality and quantity of links, however it is best not to sacrifice the quality for quantity as the quality of the site that the 'vote' or link comes from plays a key factor in the improvement of your site in the search engine rankings, due to the respect that the search engine has for that sites 'vote'.

The respect that a search engine such as Google has for a website can be identified at a high level by the PR or Page Rank a website has. Page Rank comes from a multitude of criteria found in algorithms used by Google and other Search Engines and is a rating out of 10 (10 being the best and highest quality site out there).

Having said this there are very few with a 9 or 10 Page Rank these are reserved for very few such as Google.com itself. At time of writing there are only approximately 20 Page Ranked 10 Websites in the world, including Facebook.com, whitehouse.gov, w3.org and get.adobe.com.

Link Building is known as off-site website optimisation, any good quality and effective Search Engine Optimisation Campaign should also consist of on-site optimisation which refers to content, meta data, internal links as well as several other key areas - all of which will be covered in future blog articles.

Off-site Website Optimisation consists of more than just Link Building, although Link Building is a key part of it and is actually a key part of Search Engine Optimisation in general.

There are a multitude of link building websites and directories that you can either be free or that you pay for. Usually if you are prepared to have a reciprocal link to the directory or pay a fee, then your site will be looked at and accepted more quickly.

So although the design and construction of Websites, how people use and interact with websites have changed the principles and importance of Link Building within an effective Search Engine Optimisation campaign remains the same, for the time being...

Blog 10
Email marketing or SPAM?

The fast growth of the internet means that now when the word SPAM is mentioned most people think 'unsolicited emails' instead of 'canned meat.' SPAM is associated with companies sending emails full of irrelevant information or emails that contain viruses.

The assumption that email marketing is SPAM is unfortunate as when used correctly email marketing is a fantastic tool to reach your audience and pass on information effectively.

Marketing is plagued by the argument that it is difficult to measure the effectiveness. However, email marketing can be measured by setting up analytics so you can see who has opened it, whether they have clicked on a links and been taken to the website or just deleted it.

Email marketing can drive traffic to your website by providing links to take customers to certain areas of the website. It can also remind people of your existence and raise awareness, so your company is at the top of their mind.

Because of there being no official regulations, it is easy for any company who has internet access and a list of email addresses to create a distribution list and send out an email.

Here are 5 tips on how to use email marketing as a positive tool to promote and engage customers with your company:

1. **Content**

    The content of the email should be interesting and relevant to the customers who receive it. It shouldn't be an email full of the 'hard sell' neither should it contain boring information that has no impact on the individual. This can be achieved by making sure the writer of the content has previous experience and understands this fundamental point.

2. **Compatibility**

Ok, so you have the content perfected, the distribution list of willing recipients made, you click send. But they can't view it...

Make sure that the format is compatible with their systems and the fonts used can be opened by the internet browser.

3. **Integrate**

Email marketing by itself is effective but when integrated with other marketing tools such as social media its effectiveness is drastically increased. Consumers are already involved with your company and chose to engage with it on social media sites so the next progression would be to infiltrate their inbox. They will recognise it and therefore it won't be seen as SPAM, rather as an extension of their engagement.

4. **Scheduled**

Just because email marketing is comparably cheaper than running a direct mail campaign of the same size, do not abuse this. Emails should be sent on a periodical basis to make sure they aren't over used and consequently ignored.

5. **Opt out**

Email recipients should have an option to opt out or unsubscribe. There should be a clear and easy procedure to follow which should be honored by the company. If the recipient continues to receive emails after this they will often then develop a negative association with the company.

By following the tips above and embarking on the process with a design company who has previous experience make sure that you are using email marketing to its full potential.

Blog 11
Objectives and toolkits

When working with a business all day and every day, often your focus is on making it successful, that's the whole point isn't it? You know you need to sell more products or provide your service more often in order to get money in the till, to pay fixed costs and your homes mortgage/rent. However often, taking a step back and looking how things connect together can be extremely beneficial.

The importance of setting objectives is paramount. How do you know if you have achieved what you want to if you haven't got anything to aim for?

Most businesses have the same overall aim, which is to be a success. The interesting part comes when looking at how different businesses approach this...

By setting a marketing objective such as: 'Increase sales of my product by 10% in the next 3 months' it gives your business something to aim for. It also allows you to set marketing communications objectives as ways to help you achieve them. To sell more products, more people need to know about them.

Therefore your marketing communications strategy to help achieve the above marketing objective would be: 'to increase brand awareness by 30% over the next 2 months.'

Still not getting it? No...

Your objective: To get to the other side of the river. Marketing communications objectives act as your stepping stones to get to the other side without getting wet – you wouldn't just jump in the water now would you?!

What has a website got to do with it?

Your website is one of your stepping stones, in fact it could even be a rowing boat depending on how good it is. A website offers you a fantastic opportunity to communicate with your customers. You can advertise your products, share information, discuss topics of interest, review your products, share information and engage with customers. A website is often a face of an organisation as it is possible it's the only element of the business customers will see or it is the first contact they will have with the company, hence the importance of getting it right.

Marketing communications has many tools to help achieve the task. Just like a mechanic needs spanners and torches, marketers need personal selling, advertising, public relations, direct marketing and sales promotions. When used together and for their correct use, the marketing machine will work in harmony and the products will fly off the shelves and objectives will be achieved.

So reassess your toolkit – if things are missing it might be a good time to check and replace.

Blog 12
Making Call to Actions Work

Call to Actions play a vital part on any website. Call to actions point people in the right direction and funnel them into carrying out an action with a desired outcome of some sort.

The actions that you may want to include on your site can vary depending on the service, offer or action you are trying to convey, examples may include:

- **Buy Now**
- **Sign-up Today**
- **Call us for more**
- **Read Further Info**
- **Download Now**
- **Upgrade Software**
- **Try for FREE**
- **10% Offer Today**

An effective Call to Action needs to abide by certain criteria to ensure they not only draw the user to them but ensure that they entice the user to take the necessary action you want them to, for example contacting you or signing up.

Some of the key areas to consider when integrating or planning to integrate Call to Actions are as follows:

Good use of Colour and Font

Make sure that the style of your Call to Action stands out on the website with good use of colour and font. Choose an opposite colour or one that stands out as well as ensuring that the font you use can be read easily, the last thing you want when trying to get a succinct message across is to use a font the user can't read! Obviously never rely entirely on colour, just in case you have people that are colour blind and can't see the contrast.

Effective Position of Call to Action

Think carefully about where you position your call to action on your website. Ensure it can be seen easily and clearly and is in a position that allows people to see it without hunting for it.

Ensure the Message is Clear

What do you want from the Call to Action? Do you want people to call you? Do you want people to register, join, download, view, read, stop, start, buy, do, don't, sponsor or write? Just make sure that what ever you want users to do, is clear and concise.

Make it Noticeable and Frequent

For maximum effectiveness make sure that the Call to Action is easy to see, also ensure that you use white space effectively, do not squash it into a corner or hide it with text, be proud to place the Call to Action somewhere on it's own with plenty of space around it. Also make it frequent, add it to every page so that no matter where users enter your site they can see it.

So there you have it, several key considerations to ensure that your Call to Action does not go to waste and fall by the wayside. Obviously there is one more key factor that we have not mentioned and that is track the success of the Call to Action, put a process or analytics in place to track and understand how well your Call to Action is doing and the positive effect on your business as a result.

Blog 13
Ways to build loyalty online

The great 'social' media.

For many of us we have added all our friends on Facebook, our business contacts on LinkedIn and keep followers regularly up to date with our actions, pictures and funny quotes on Twitter. But what's the different for businesses and does it actually matter?

Believe it or not, having fans on your Facebook page, likes on your activity updates and retweets of your link is rather important and a good indicator as to the general feeling towards your brand. It is all fine and dandy having them, but how can you make sure they keep coming back? Did they just join your fan page by chance or are they loyal to your brand?

One of the ways to increase loyalty online is to give visitors reasons to come back. Engage with them, make them feel welcome and comfortable in the knowledge that if they leave a comment you will follow it up with a 'thank you' or engage into a dialogue with them. There is the famous phrase of, 'It's like talking to a brick wall' and we all know that it's unfair to expect that.

By building up an emotional connection with customers your brand/business will be differentiated from competitors.

They are called 'social' media platforms for a reason!

Allow the company to have a personality, a persona that ties in with the rest of the business and its main objectives. However do ensure that various members of the team are able to keep the sites updated and keep it integrated. Otherwise your loyal fans will notice the difference and might not be loyal anymore!

It is important to note that the 'personality' of the brand needs to be cohesive with the whole business and is better suited to certain sectors of business than others. For example Citigroup are unlikely to post an update on Twitter giving their opinion on the latest Katie Price/Jordan scandal, whereas a public relations company might.

Another top tip is to make sure that up to date information is posted when and where it is needed. Main websites should be easy to navigate and updated on a regular basis. There is nothing worse than sites where nothing changes for months or in some cases brands have had inappropriate and brand damaging pictures posted on the site by external spammers.

Customers want to see new content and pictures, something to come back and look for. In terms of navigation, there is no point in having to search through hundreds of subtitles and links to find something that should be on the front page, customers are likely to get bored and go elsewhere. One of the great advantages of online content is it is fast and easy – so make sure yours is.

Customers often find it easier to make repeat purchases so give them what they want and they are likely to stay loyal!

Blog 14
Using Royalty Free Image Stock

A picture paints a thousand words. This is certainly the case with good quality stock image or a digital photo.

There isn't a modern website designed now days that doesn't make good use of stock imagery and photos available to them online. Carefully chosen stock imagery can dramatically improve the look and feel of a website and transform what would otherwise have been a very bland and unimpressive looking site into a professional, vivid and eye catching one.

Within the past decade it has become much easier to access images and photos online but with the birth of Royalty Free Image Stock sites use of digital images has rocketed.

Purchasing Stock Imagery

There are many websites to purchase your images from and below are our top 5 Royalty Free Image Stock Sites:

1. Fotolia - www.fotolia.co.uk
2. Getty Images - www.gettyimages.co.uk
3. iStockphoto - www.istockphoto.com
4. Juniper Images - www.jupiterimages.com
5. Shutterstock Photo - www.Shutterstock.com

Even though the stock images are very cheap and can be attained easily after signing up with an image stock website, you need to ensure that you purchase the correct license for the type of work you intend to use the image it for. There are now quite strict guidelines on purchasing the correct license for the image and this tends to depend on the purpose and whether you intend to re-sell the image on a piece of work or a template and if so what quantity.

For more info on the licensing rules you would need to view the respective terms on the stock site you were purchasing from.

Selling Stock Imagery

If you have an eye for catching the perfect picture on your camera then why not set-up an account with an image stock site and sell your images? Each and every image stock site will have certain criteria that needs to be satisfied in order for the images to be shown and sold via their site.

The sort of criteria that would need to be adhered to before your images are accepted consist of areas like: quality, resolution, subject matter, legal, copyright, uniqueness and other various image and photo quality conformity.

We will be writing more specifically about various useful tips and advice on the use and selling of image stock in future.

Blog 15
Online Vs Offline Networking

Ooooo the night has finally arrived of the networking event, you have waited for this night for weeks. You have your name badge clipped onto your freshly ironed shirt, your cup of tea or coffee in your hand and you are stood in a room full of people – some of which you have seen before and others you are yet to meet. You have a vague idea of what they do and most people look as nervous as you...

Your friend is at home, no make-up on, wearing tracksuit bottoms and a big t-shirt. Their laptop is in front of them by chance, TV on in the background and they have just 'networked' with the head of a worldwide PR agency...

How did that happen?!

Networking has been revolutionised by the Internet. No longer are you required to attend events to mix with a group of people similar to yourself, the Internet has effectively made the world smaller. Online Networking is extremely convenient as you are able to network with someone on the other side of the world at any time of day, you do it in your own time and your own pace and if you don't want to speak to anyone – you don't have to!

Twitter and LinkedIn have opened up the world of work, making it easy to search for people who may be of interest as you are able to search by sector, name and company. People are now more accessible than ever, how else would you be able to engage in correspondence with industry leaders who you might never meet?

Twitter chats are also a popular way to meet with people who share similar interests, for example for PR it would be #commschat.

With online networking you don't waste time probing them with questions, you can find out exactly who they are, what they do, their current and past positions and sometimes even their relationship status with the click of a mouse.

However it is important that offline networking has its advantages, nothing is as good as a face to face meeting. Seeing someone in the flesh gives you endless advantages, you can assess body language and facial expressions and answers are always in real time. Where has the art of conversation gone? What is wrong with asking people what they do? Spending time with people, asking them questions and expressing an interest can sometimes mean that you forge longer and stronger relationships in the long run. Also it must not be forgotten that meanings can be changed over email or tweets and let's be honest....just how much information can you put into 140 characters?

Networking is probably one of the easiest ways to market your business and as with most tools in the marketing toolbox it is much more effective when combined with other tools so use a combination of offline and online networking, strike a balance.

Just make sure that when you do it, either online or offline, you remember that you represent the business at all times. However, one of the main advantages with online networking is that there is a delete button...if only we had that in real life!

Blog 16
Why should I use Linked-In?

Imagine your address book contained up to date contact details of colleagues and directors old and new without having to phone them and check regularly. Imagine being able to see CV's of potential employees complete with recommendations from previous employers. Imagine gaining new contacts from existing ones without meeting face to face. Now you can...

LinkedIn is defined as a business orientated social networking site. Founded by Reid Hoffman in 2002 and launched in May 2003 it enables users to keep an online address book full of old, existing and future connections with pictures and contact details.

Users who register can build up their contact list by searching for contacts via name, company or email address. They can also follow and research companies of interest, discover potential jobs and gain introductions from their connections contact list.

This notion of 'virtual networking' is one of the benefits of LinkedIn – and one that I have found extremely useful. From their office, home or on the move users are able to 'connect with' directors of companies at the click of a mouse. It is a spider web effect with the user at the centre.

The website also offers a great alternative to keeping in touch with colleagues without adding them on Facebook, which can sometimes create problems - please see 'Social Networking - business or pleasure?'

Your LinkedIn profile appears in search results when your name is typed into Google so can be used by potential employers to see your job history and any recommendations that you may have received. Many users include a link to their profile on their CV so that employers can look at the information available online.

LinkedIn offers some fantastic benefits to users so start making the most of it today.

Blog 17
Tips for surviving a recession

For those that hadn't noticed, our country is emerging from one of the worst recessions of all time. Unless you have buried your head in the sand, been trapped in a cave or been living on your own private island with no TV or means of communication (in which case, feel free to share with me), you might have noticed that disposable income has reduced and competition between businesses and debts have increased...

Consumers are now placing emphasis on different factors when purchasing products. Price is extremely important, with less disposable income customers are being increasingly savvy with the money they do have. Talking about money is no longer taboo and people are openly discussing details of their finances with their friends and family. Now when customers find a bargain they are proud to tell their reference groups. In an uncertain world consumers are wanting to take control of their lives and are expressing this through their power over their purchases.

So what can companies do?

Return to their core values or develop some new ones

Consumers are looking for purchases to fulfil a higher need of self-actualisation, they want to feel as if they are doing something good. Whether that be for the environment or for farmers in foreign countries. Businesses that embark on cause related marketing will introduce the consumer to another reason as to why consumers should buy their product. Sustainability is moving up the agenda for consumers – so make sure it's moving up yours.

Transparency

There has been a marked reduction in consumer's levels of trust of big companies and institutions so transparency is key. Engage with consumers and give them truthful information.

Engage and encourage consumer involvement

CGM (consumer generated media), UGM (user generated media) or UGC (user generated content) – Whatever you call it, encourage consumers to take the lead in your marketing efforts. If they have used the product and service get them to tell their friends over social networking sites, write a blog about it or tweet. Consumers increasingly trust others who have been in contact with the product or service over so-called 'experts'.

Get close to consumers

Gone are the days when transactional marketing is enough. Build a relationship with consumers and make them feel special. Relationship marketing is key in building brand loyalty, which is vital to market share and revenue.

Be more creative

Consumers are becoming increasingly dubious of believing adverts and obvious marketing techniques so mix in more creative methods such as PR, guerrilla marketing and expeditionary marketing. Add some more tools to your tool kit...

Environmental scanning

Trends are changing and will continue to shift for years to come so keep an ear close to the ground and keep up to date with trends and patterns in consumer behaviour.

The effects of the recession will be felt for years to come and consumer behaviour may have changed forever. Consumers have realised that they can be sensible with money and don't always have to purchase products that they don't need. In the words of Karl Lagerfeld, 'Bling is over', being thrifty is fashionable.

Learn it and embrace it. Don't get left behind...

Blog 18
Top Website Design Tips – Part 1

So....What are the most important tips or bits of advice that we can provide you with regards to making the most of your Company Website to ensure you get value for money.

1. **Do your Research**

    Make sure that you put enough time into carrying out some research. If you have a website already then how can you improve it, were you getting what you wanted from your old site? If not, why not? Who are your Competitors? Who are your Audience and who would you ideally like to be getting to the site? Is your site for showcase purposes, to be used as a brochureware website or an online shop? All of these questions and more need to be asked before you even approach anyone to build it for you. Be very clear on what you would like the website to achieve for you, who your competitors are and who your audience is. Simple points I know, but its amazing how many people do not give it any thought at all then wonder why their beautifully designed website is not performing as they would have liked.

2. **Website Requirements**

    So you fathomed out some initial ideas via the research you have carried out, know who your audience is, who your competitors are and what you would like from your site. So now you need to outline what those requirements are. These website requirements will act as the bench mark for you to look back on and assess whether your website has been designed to the spec you required. So many people rush in before they have defined exactly what it is they want from their website? Again very basic points, but these will really help you throughout the development of your site as well as qualifying the end product against your initial website requirements.

3. **Succinct but Sexy**

    Once you have decided who will build your site (which should be no 2.5), we come to the look and feel of the site. Many website designers will tell you that this is the most important element of a site due to the fact that if people see the site and are put off by the look of it, they will just go elsewhere.. Well yes, there is a lot of truth in that statement, however it is not the only element that must be treated with importance. A website's design will obviously be driven by the industry and audience you are targeting, so ensure that you take this into consideration when designing the site.

4. **Content, Content, Content**

    Just as important, if not more important than the design is content, after all content is King! The content that you use within your website should be succinct and descriptive, it should contain key words that you would like to be found on within

Search Engines.. Not too many as it will just dilute the effectiveness of the content with regards to SEO. Also keep it fresh.. Ensure that your content is kept up to date, changed and added to on a regular basis via news and blog articles.

5. **Calls to actions**

   Ensure that users or customers can easily get access to you, via telephone numbers, feedback forms, email addresses, contact forms or live chat methods. Make these methods available from all pages on the site to prevent the user from having to keep navigating to and from the contact page (presuming you have one). Call to actions are yet another sometimes overlooked element to any website. Make sure you make it easy for customers to contact you, this is vital..

So there you have it – the first of 2 parts to our top tips for designing a website, part 2 to follow..

Blog 19
Top Website Design Tips – Part 2

Here is the second part of our top website design tips blog..

6. **Search Engine optimisation in mind from the Outset..**

   SEO, Search Engine Optimisation, Web Optimisation – whatever you call it, you need it and it needs to be part of the way you think about and construct your site from day 1. Search Engine Optimisation (SEO) can be categorised into several key areas some on-site and some off-site. On-site SEO elements consist of (in no particular order) meta tag optimisation, good content, internal links, fresh content and blog articles, alt text, good HTML / CSS code structure, W3C web compliance, Header tags and sitemap. There are plenty more but these several points are the very least you can do to aid your SEO.

7. **User Experience**

    Your site is now looking good, it has all the call to actions necessary, has been designed with SEO in mind and has great content! That's it isn't it... Well no, not exactly, what about user experience? It may be the best designed site ever and be well optimised but if the user finds it hard to either move around the site or purchase your product, this will let all of the other elements down. You need to design the website from a user's point of view. Throughout the designing of your site you need to be mindful of how the user will look, travel, use and buy from your site. This needs to be as easy and as hassle free as possible!

8. **Keep it Fresh!**

    So you have put a lot of time and effort into building the site and have launched the site.. Probably the worst thing you can do now (apart from not promote it) is to not update or add regular content to the site. Users may visit your site once but if there is nothing that changes then they will soon get bored, also in terms of Search Engine Optimisation this is also not good. Search Engines do keep track of how frequently your site is updated and will treat that site accordingly in terms of the frequency at which it visits and updates its search results.

9. **Post Launch Maintenance..**

    So your site has gone live, now what do you do? How do you maintain the site, who maintains it and how? Had you planned for the post launch maintenance up front? If not then it could be difficult and very time consuming to update and edit your own site. Now days there are many Content Management Systems (CMS) or sites on the market, these are good if you need to update on a regular basis. If you do not need to update on a regular basis then CMS may not be required, however see point 8 - Keep it Fresh!

10. Analytics

Analytics are one of the most useful and valuable tools to be used in conjunction with your website once you have launched it. Once you have spent your valuable money and time on your site, you want to be able to measure and track how successful your site is in the way of visitors, products sold and pages viewed. What you can't track now days isn't worth knowing. Analytics need to be hooked in from the outset to ensure that you can see and track how well your new website is doing, from there you can begin to understand the trends of your visitors, why they are visiting your site and why possibly they are not. Using the website statistics you can continue to tweak and tailor your site to suit the trends and in turn generate more interest and sales, and so the cycle continues.

So there you have it! Our top website design tips covered over 2 parts. This will provide you with the fundamental tools to design a website that works for you.

Blog 20
Do people feel safe buying online?

The UK leads the rest of Europe in terms of the amount spent online with the biggest sales on books, DVD's, leisure and travel. Sales are estimated to reach £56 billion by 2014 so with figures like that is it still possible that people are dubious about purchasing items online?

Department stores are popular because consumers are able to get everything from under one roof. Online is exactly the same but with an endless amount of goods, consumers can sit on their chairs or sofas, order whatever they would like from underwear to remote controlled cars and it can be done 24/7.

Reasons that people worry about buying goods online vary. Some worry about their credit card information getting into the wrong hands, others worry about their personal information being used in a fraudulent way. Certain individuals are simply intimidated by the whole process and others, particularly younger people, don't want to wait for the delivery of the goods and see it was a waste of time.

E-tailing offers different benefits depending on what the individual may want. Online individuals can:
- Reserve and collect
- Purchase and get it delivered
- Search for the best price - three out of five consumers think that the prices offered online are better than the ones in store
- Buy online because they don't want the human interaction
- Some items are not available in store - the internet has a limitless shop front

Statistics show that women are more dubious than men when purchasing goods online with many of them abandoning a sale if the website isn't working as they expected. 33% of consumers worry about security and 41% prefer using a well-known retailer when buying online.

To make customers feel comfortable websites need to provide evidence that they can be trusted with consumers' personal details and make them feel at ease. There is however 20% of consumers who would be happy buying from a website they haven't heard of. Leading retailers, such as Argos and Marks and Spencer, have begun integrating their channels in order to make the customers experience seamless and to reassure the 80% of consumers who prefer a website they recognise.

With generations of children being taught that ordering items online is convenient and the methods becoming even more efficient the number of people purchasing goods will undoubtedly increase. There will however always be people who prefer not to purchase certain items online but without those people where would it leave the high street?

Blog 21
How to take the perfect picture

So you have decided that you want to go it alone, this might be because you have previous experience, because your budget doesn't stretch to employing a photographer or because stock photography is not fit for this purpose.

But where on Earth do you start? Whether you have never picked up a camera before or are 'experienced' in taking pictures on nights out, by following these top tips you will have a picture you are pleased with:

- **Vision**

    You should have an idea of the type of photograph that you want to achieve. What will it contain? Are the people in it natural or posed? Does your picture contain people at all? What impression do you want to give? Draw an example of the main shapes in the picture and work out how you can achieve this.

- **Location, Location, Location**

    Where are you planning on taking the pictures? Outside, if so be wary of the weather. Inside? In a studio? Rent somewhere? In the office? All of these considerations should be taken into account. If the picture is to be taken in public then be careful not to get anybody else's face in it without their written permission. Is there anything that could get into the picture that you wouldn't want?

- **Have the correct equipment**

    Depending on what the picture is to be used for, ensure that the equipment you have is correct for the purpose. If you need an image with a high resolution then you may need to use an SLR camera instead of a standard digital camera.

However if the image is to be used on Facebook or uploaded on Twitter then a digital camera would be more than adequate.

- **Lighting**

    Lighting is an important element in pictures and can make the difference between a good picture and a great picture. Artificial or natural? From the front or behind? Varying the light source can change the look and feel of the picture so play around with it and see which suits your vision best.

- **Take more than one**

    Don't just take one, take a few! We all know the saying: 'Just in case' so ensure that you don't miss your opportunity for a great shot by not taking more than one. While you have everything in place make the most and take as many pictures as you can. The beauty of digital cameras means that you are no longer 'wasting' film so click away.

Most importantly, have fun with it and be in charge of the camera. Imagine your vision and get as close to it as you can. There is no harm done trying things out, so be daring!

Blog 22
How to make your site easy to view

One of the top features that visitors want from a website is for it to be 'easy to navigate'. However even now, some websites aren't providing this and are instead giving visitors large blocks of text, nowhere to click, pop up videos every two seconds and a contact page that attempts to open up Outlook instead of simply stating an email address... By remembering the tips below you will make your website one of the sites that visitors find easy to navigate:

Understand your visitors...

Put yourself in their shoes - think about what they want and how they would like it presenting. The best way to do this is to ask them! Carry out some market research as to what they would like or look at, how similar businesses have done it and ask yourself whether their presentation has been successful. It is also important to understand that behavior is different when consumers are looking at a webpage online from when they see an advert in a newspaper or magazine. Their eye movements differ and they are more like to quickly scan the page to see if there is anything of interest – bear this is mind when formatting your website.

... And give them what they want!

Websites should act as a place where visitors can find answers to the questions they have about the business, they should not confuse visitors so they have more questions to ask than before they looked at the site!

Don't overload pages...

It is easy to overload pages with images and text, after all there is a lot of information to get across. You are not 100% sure as to the exact information your visitor wants, so it surely it seems logical to tell them everything as soon as they click onto your page? No, don't bombard them with everything the business does and offers on the first page. Visitors to websites don't mind looking around and clicking on different pages, as long as the pages are clearly titled and contain the information they promise. Also it is often more effective to leave space to draw attention to what is important.

...So avoid big blocks of text.

It is rare that visitors to your site will want to see a blog block of text, visitors to websites like to be able to scan the page and pick up information. The nature of the web means that visitors are always looking at something else and their attention span is considerably lower than usual, so cater for this. Don't give the visitor a big block of text to decipher, instead spilt up your text with images, use different fonts or use pagination if required.

By ensuring that your website is easy to navigate visitors will see it as an easy and reliable place to find the information they are looking for. If you provide visitors with this they are more likely to visit your site again.

Blog 23
The key to effective web optimisation

Web Optimisation, SEO, Search Engine Optimisation, Organic SEO, Site SEO, whatever you call it, it has now become a key part of both the build and promotion of any website. In order to generate visitors, good search engine rankings and potentially revenue it is critical!

It is no secret that there are many companies now entering the Search Engine Optimisation field, but what makes the difference between just good Web Optimisation and excellent SEO that gives you results?

Well there are several key areas that will help your Website Optimisation online and using all of these techniques together will collectively allow you to gain the edge for your chosen key words and in turn produce excellent results in the rankings.

Key words, key words, key words

Key words are really important, if you do not put enough thought or research into the key words you are looking to be found on, then you are off on the wrong foot straight away.. The Key words you choose will act as the foundation to much of the Web Optimisation work going forward. Key words are the lynch pin to any effective SEO campaign.

There are many research and analysis tools out there to help you choose the best key words for your website, so ensure you put the time in up front to choose between 5 – 10 key words that will be the basis for your site optimisation.

On-site Optimisation

With regards to on-site optimsation there are several important areas to consider. Firstly Meta Tags. Now even though these are not seen as important as they used to be, they are important. More so to give users an idea on what the page is about within search engine results as well as a useful set of instructions for Search Engine's with regards to indexing. Secondly website analytics. In order for you to gauge how well the optimising of your website is going as well as the areas you need to improve you will need to hook in a good analytics package. Try www.google.com/analytics. Thirdly and most importantly content, after all content is king! Ensure that the content on your website is well constructed, has a suitable scattering of your chosen key words that are preferably linked or nestled in header tags and finally that it does not read like a chunk of text written specifically for search engines.

Off-site Optimisation

Off-site optimisation is just as important as on site and can also be summed up with several key areas. Firstly, Link Building, this has had good and bad press over the years and people have differing techniques and theories regarding the best way to achieve good results. Some people say it's more important to have quantity of links over quality and some say quality of links are far more important than quantity. Well the truth is that a bit of both wouldn't hurt... However we believe that quality of links, meaning the quality of the site that you are linking from, is most important. It is better to start slow and get some good links in place with sites that have a good Page Rank rather than look to get many links very quickly, this may even have an adverse effect.

Secondly Online PR is a must! If you have a product, service, niche idea or just something to shout about then write it down and spread the news. There are now a multitude of news and online blogging style websites that allow you to share with other people...vast amounts of people... So write a good article and get it out there. Preferably make this a regular thing as well.

Search Media Optimsiation SMO

Finally it has been the buzz word for the past few years – SMO or Search Media Optimisation. This involves all of the social networking websites such as Facebook, Twitter, Bebo, Linked In, MySpace – these are just a small selection of the most well known ones – for a more extensive list visit this A – Z link of Social Networking websites: http://en.wikipedia.org/wiki/List_of_social_networking_websites.

So what's the craze? Well you can either look at our latest Social Networking Blog articles:

Twitter - What's it all about?
Social Networking - Business or Pleasure?
Facebook - What's it all about?

Or you can just ask any one of the millions upon millions or people using them. For any business not harnessing the power of social media they can consider themselves well and truly left behind.

Social Networking websites used to be seen as a form of informal social media method for youngsters in chat between each other and share things, it has come on a long way since then. Used effectively Social Networking not only benefit, but boost the online marketing of any website. If you're not using it start today!

Blog 24
When is a good time to rebrand?

Rebranding your company can be a daunting thought, especially when things seem to be fine the way they are – why fix something that's not broke? But rebranding doesn't need to be something that you enter with dread it can be a positive thing and carry with it very positive consequences...

There are many reasons that companies may *want* to rebrand and also reasons that mean they *need* to.

A common reason for a company considering a rebrand is if the current brand isn't doing particularly well or as well as it could be. If you have tried everything else, a rebrand maybe exactly what you need to refresh your brand and boost staff morale!

Your company has been through a crisis and consumers might have lost faith. A rebrand would be a fantastic way of moving on from such an incident. However it would be naive to think that by simply changing your name and logo you can shake off any responsibility, a rebrand should be part of an overall crisis management strategy.

If there have been changes in the market your company might be out of touch. A rebrand would bring your company up to date and allow it run alongside consumers and competitors in this fast moving market place. If you want to diversify into a new market area or reposition in an existing one, a rebrand might be helpful in aiding this transition as your existing brand image might not be transferable to new areas.

However company's mustn't forget the importance of existing brand equity, if your company has customers there must be something they value about your existing brand and it would be a mistake to ignore this. Plus many think that 'rebranding' is changing the name of the business, using a different logo, ordering some new branded pens and updating the look of the website. Admittedly these tasks are included in a rebrand but staff are also involved so ensure that they reflect the values and changes of the new brand image you are trying to project. In such a challenging business environment you need to stand out so if you identify the need or the want to rebrand take the plunge...it's not as scary as you think and the benefits could be great!

Blog 25
What is Expeditionary Marketing?

Expeditionary Marketing is not a trek along the Great Wall of China or even a climb to the top of Mount Kilimanjaro. You don't have to travel to the Amazon and navigate your way through the unknown forests and discover dangerous native tribes. Expeditionary Marketing can all be done from the comfort of your organisation's HQ, your office or your home...

Society has changed due to many factors, from reductions in the amount of disposable income that your customers have to rising costs of running their homes. Consumers are becoming increasingly media savvy and have been for the past few decades, they are no longer guaranteed to seek information about certain products. No longer can marketers rely on a television advert on a popular channel, a couple of adverts in a generic magazine and a leaflet through a consumers' front door. New innovative methods are emerging as businesses look for opportunities to approach and target new markets and gain valuable market share.

A new discipline is emerging and it is essential that companies who want to be successful at least acknowledge its existence. Entrepreneurial Marketing is based on 7 key principles:

- Pro-activeness
- Calculated Risk taking
- Innovativeness
- Opportunity focus
- Resource leveraging
- Customer intensity
- Value creation

Expeditionary marketing is one of the tools in the kit of entrepreneurial marketing. It acknowledges that failure might take place, but it is a risk worth taking. It is based on the question of:

1. **Whether your business is there to simply serve customers and create new markets?**
2. **Do your marketing efforts follow consumer's wants and needs or does it lead them in new directions?**

If you are still not with it then let us use an example:

The Apple brand is extremely entrepreneurial in its approach to business. They are a brand that are willing to put themselves out there and take risks. Who would have ever thought that the IPod would have made such as impact? It is extremely hard to find a household without an IPod and even if an individual already had an mp3 player they would often purchase an IPod anyway. Just think to yourself, was there a market for a touch screen computer that allowed consumers to play games, view pictures, browse the internet, edit documents and download some pointless applications? No. There wasn't. Apple didn't identify a specific audience that needed these benefits, they launched a product and caused enough of a buzz around it through various forms of marketing and PR that consumers were convinced they needed one and it was a given that hardcore Apple Loyalists would purchase one anyway. Clever hey?!

For companies like Apple who are in the fast moving world of technology it is easier to create new products and pose them to consumers as new gadgets are being invented all the time. But could every business benefit from expeditionary market to a certain degree? By looking beyond serving consumers and venturing into the unknown your business might discover something new or tap into a new target audience you never knew you had. It was said at the beginning of the article that your business wasn't required to enter the unknown forest of the Amazon, but to a certain extent it is. The world is a big place with many unknowns, so go and explore, you never know that native tribe you find might love your product...

Blog 26
Colourful branding for a colourful company!

Marketing is a way to get your business known, it helps to give your company brand awareness, and often it can be used as a method of differentiation. Not all businesses want to market in the same ways as their competitors and in a market full of companies offering similar services and products, a company's approach to marketing can make all the difference.

One of the best ways to be noticed amongst your target audience is to get to know them. Academics call them 'salient beliefs', these are the attributes consumers are looking for and if activated they allow consumers to form overall attitudes on the product. These attitudes can make the difference between a consumer choosing your product over a competitors.

But how do you get to know your consumers?

Market research is an option and has been used by many companies to create successful campaigns. T-mobile is living proof that identifying consumers attitudes about a situation and appealing to them in your marketing communications can make you stand out. They carried out market research at the beginning of the recession and found that consumers were turning to friends and family, spending increasing amounts of time with them and they also found that unplanned get-togethers were becoming more popular. This research led Saatchi and Saatchi to create the 'Life's for sharing' campaign and the famous Flashmob in Victoria station. It quickly created a buzz online and became a viral marketing campaign as people had captured the moment on their phones and uploaded it straight to Youtube.com therefore emphasising the role of 'sharing'. Footage was also made into a TV advert and stills used for billboard, magazine and newspaper adverts. By appealing to their customers current attitudes and almost saying 'we understand and we can help'

T-mobile contract sales increased by half compared to the same period the year before.

Another way to understand consumers is to put yourself in their shoes. What do they want? How would you like to be told about if you were them? What sort of media do they use? If your target audience are fans of social media then focus on that and do something creative, let them take the lead in sharing the links and encourage them to make spoof adverts, offer to put the best on the brand website. Think about what your customers would respond to and cater to it. After all if you can make your customers feel special they are more likely to remain loyal to your brand.

The best advice that can be given for companies not wanting to do the same as competitors is to try something new, take a new slant on an old idea and don't jump on every bandwagon that goes past. Being different is bound to bring with it potential dangers and others may think your ideas are off the wall but do bear in mind: people used to believe the world was flat and those that suggested differently were the 'weird' ones...

Blog 27
Top 5 social networking websites

There is debate as to what makes a website 'top' is it number of people using it? How it ranks on satisfaction? Ease of use? Is it the most well known?

The popularity of a website often varies between countries due to various factors such as: how it fits in with the culture, the ease of usage, how it is represented in the media and the rules and regulations associated with it.

However the following sites are popular across the UK and some of them on a worldwide basis.

Facebook

Facebook is by far the most popular and well known social networking site in the world. Known across the world it has a film based on its creation and its founder is now one of the richest men in the world. Not bad to say it was the idea of a University student...

MySpace

Popular with bands as a way to showcase their material, MySpace is another well known social networking site across the world. Its focus is on entertainment rather than information on individuals, it offers a great way for bands to share information with fans such as tour dates and new releases.

Twitter

What can you say with 140 characters?! This was the initial reaction from many people, however Twitter has become an extremely successful social networking site where people share links, pictures and opinions. The question is now what can't be said in 140 characters?

LinkedIn

LinkedIn offers an easy and effective way for individuals to create an online CV and 'link in' with others who share the same job interest. It offers an alternative way of being recruited and allows likeminded individuals to share thoughts and ideas.

Bebo

Bebo stands for 'Blog Early, Blog Often' and is traditionally associated with younger people. Its layout is similar to Facebook and the idea behind it is the same as it offers users a chance to share pictures, comments and videos.

Blog 28
How has Marketing changed over the past 10 years?

The year 2000 was meant to bring many changes. Everyone would begin wearing silver space suits, flying around the sky in private space ships or on a more sombre note there was the possibility of the end of the World due to the Millennium bug... In reality none of this has happened...

But over the past 10 years marketing is one thing that has changed. Many of the changes may have seemed insignificant, but those businesses that retain a continued increase in customers need to keep ahead of these trends.

With most households having internet access and new methods of communication with consumers have opened up to marketers. Marketers are now able to use tools such as social networking, email marketing and viral videos to target consumers. In turn this has created the possibility of 2 way symmetrical communication with consumers which can aid with evaluations of campaigns.

Contrary to speculation we aren't experiencing 'the death of traditional media as we know it' – it is true that print media has experienced a decline in its popularity but in my opinion print media will always have a place so long as the digital divide exists. Marketers must understand that there needs to be a balance and a mixture of marketing methods used.

Consumers now see advertising for what it is and are able to see through transparent campaigns. Marketers need to treat consumers with the respect they deserve and mix old methods with the new, to offer cohesive yet interesting marketing campaign.

In some ways audiences have become fragmented with consumers having higher expectations and increasing control over their purchases. This has led to a rise in the number of niche television programmes, magazines and websites. Consequently marketers have the option to target specific audiences with tailored media vehicles. Initially it could be thought that this would make marketers jobs easier, which is in part true, however it is now increasingly difficult to decide where to focus already tight resources to get the best results.

Companies now face competition on a global scale so it is even more important to take part in regular SWOT analysis. Businesses need to ensure that they aren't lost in the crowded market place and are in customers brand repertoires.

Society has changed over the past 10 years so it would be naive to believe that marketing should have stayed the same. It is important to track and measure changes in society and make sure that your companies marketing strategies meet the current wants and needs.

If you were to take just one piece of advice from this article it would be:

Don't sell consumers two pieces of wood when they could have a lighter...keep up with the times!

Blog 29
How important is a company website?

It's midnight on a Sunday night and a customer wants to find out where the nearest store is or whether your company stocks a certain product. Imagine being able to provide that customer with all the information they need without having to get out of bed and tell them.

A website provides you with this opportunity - It rarely takes sick days, works 24 hours a day and 7 days a week and it's even willing to work on Christmas day...

Customers often use a company website as their first point of contact with the organisation, it creates an impression of your company straight away and can sometimes make the decision as to whether the customer wants to interact with your company or not.

Benefits of having a well designed website include:
- International recognition of your company.
- Websites can often be less expensive that traditional media. Online there is no need to pay for reprinting of literature if there have been changes to any information.
- They are convenient for customers as they are able to access the information they need wherever and whenever they want to.
- You website acts as an online identity – no doubt your competitors will be online so pitch up beside them and don't miss out on valued custom.
- Gives the opportunity for increased sales – customers are more likely to buy if procedures are simple and quick. Plus some customers might discover you by using online search engines so might not have known your company existed otherwise.
- Websites can be used as a promotional tool – a successful website can raise awareness of your company and be used as an online brochure showcasing your products in a limitless showroom. Printing costs can also be cut as literature can direct people to the website.
- A website hosts the ability to update information quickly and efficiently.

On the downside it could be said that the internet is just a fad, but can you really afford to miss out on such a profitable trend? As you can be certain your competitors aren't...

Overall it IS important that your company has a website as customers use it as a source of information about your company, a place to purchase your products and it offers you company endless opportunities to communicate with your customers. However it is important to note that a good website design is extremely important, the reason many websites fail to produce results is because of bad design. Good web designers understand the need for websites to engage users and stimulate interest and often web design is not as expensive as first thought.

Blog 30
How often should I be sending my e-shots?

Providing you have followed the rules of permission marketing, your customers have asked to hear from you and if your newsletters have been written properly they will be of some interest to the reader. But how often do you send them out? Every day? Every week? Every month?

It could be likened to speaking to a friend, if they have something interesting to say you don't mind when they contact you but if they ring you every day and tell you something relatively boring then you begin to dread their phone call and if possible you attempt to 'unsubscribe' from the friendship...

If you are a business, individuals find it much easier to unsubscribe to your e-shots than they do to cut off from a friend so unfortunately the odds are against you!

It would be simple to recommend that businesses sent their mail shots out every month as that would ensure customers wouldn't forget about you and hopefully there would be enough interesting information to be included in the e-shot itself. However if your business is fast paced, evolving on a regular basis and in touch with consumers regularly why not give them more regular updates? It could be that once a week or once a fortnight would be a better option for your business as if you left it a whole month you could have missed many opportunities to alert customers to good offers and new information.

So as usual, it depends!

When you send out e-shots depends completely on the individual business, but by following these basic rules it will ensure your database doesn't dwindle:

1) Ask your customers how often they would like an e-shot.
2) Measure click through rates and see if e-shots are a valuable communication tool for your business, if not there may be better ways to utilise your marketing budget.
3) Keep a similar format – that way recipients know what to expect and can easily navigate the email.
4) Make sure you offer different formats, as some formats aren't compatible with certain types of browsers – nothing worse than spending time and money when a customer can't even open it...
5) Don't be afraid to try something different!

Blog 31
How to approach business like an entrepreneur

We all know the great success stories of the likes of Lord Sugar, Duncan Bannatyne and Anita Roddick. Those that started their business from scratch, the 'true' entrepreneurs. But how easy is it to apply some entrepreneurial thinking into the running of your business?

Easy Peasy!

According to many of the textbooks, including Schindehutte's Rethinking Marketing, there are seven underlying characteristics to an entrepreneurial marketing approach:

1. Pro-activeness

Entrepreneurs are always taking part in environmental scanning and looking towards the marketing mix for elements to change to keep up with the fast moving market place. Changes in the market place aren't viewed negatively, they are seen as opportunities. Opportunities to gain some new customers and please existing ones even more. Set aside some time everyday to have a look outside of the office walls and see what others are doing, be proactive with your business and seize every opportunity that you can, it is rare that things will be given to you, so it is essential that you go and seek them.

2. Obsession with opportunity

The recession has happened? Check. We are still feeling the effects? Check. This is a fact that everyone knows, but it's the entrepreneurs that are doing something about it. They never let their minds stop working and thinking of new places to take their business. Other people's mistakes offer them opportunities on a plate. Make sure that you use every negative situation as a positive experience as often opportunities can come from the strangest of places!

3. Calculated Risk taking

Entrepreneurs are not scared of taking risks, but neither do they enter into unfamiliar territory without either previous knowledge or some sort of reasoning behind their choices. Resources are managed in ways that mean they can be withdrawn from certain projects and committed to them with extreme speed. They work with other businesses and take part in 'strategic alliances' to further their influence and use others resources. Is it possible for you to limit the amount of full time staff you employ and draw on a larger part time team for a variety of skills? There are some areas of your business that will work out and others that won't...that's life, however do make sure that with any new venture you limit the amount of resources you commit.

4. Resource leveraging

In short, resource leveraging is 'doing more with less'. Entrepreneurs do not allow themselves to be hemmed in by the resources currently at their disposal, they focus on the ideal and organise the resources they do have in a way that allows them to achieve it. They are able to persuade other businesses to allow them to use their resources without them realising and they recognise resources within people and areas that others haven't. Have a closer look at the office junior who is doing your filing, they might have a bright idea lurking in their heads, so encourage everyone in the business to brainstorm and allow yourself to be approachable to new ideas from any member of staff. Think about any strategic alliances that you could build with other businesses in order to utilise their resources such as staff and office space as your own.

5. Innovativeness

These entrepreneurs do not just serve the customer, they lead them. They are often ahead of their competitors with developments in technology or advances in their product or service. Managers themselves champion new ideas and actively encourage creativeness on the part of consumers and employees. Always be thinking of the next big thing, monitor what your competitors are doing and make sure you don't get left behind. If you can be the first, then go for it!

6. Customer intensity

The emphasis is on the consumer. Entrepreneurs build relationships with their customers and often use them for advice and ideas. After all they are the users of your product so if they are happy, sales will rise. Smart huh?! Entrepreneurs use the knowledge they build of their consumers to anticipate their needs and wants in order to serve them more successfully. Advertisements often use emotional rather than rational triggers. Relationship marketing is important in the current economic climate, if you build a relationship with your customer they are more likely to remain loyal to you. Put yourself in your customers shoes and experience your product or service, that way you will see what you can do better.

7. Value creation

Consumers get more than just the core product when they purchase it from an entrepreneur. They are willing to travel further to use the service despite there being one only a few yards down the road because of the experience they receive. There are emotional ties between consumers and businesses and entrepreneurs realise this and use it to their advantage.

It is important to mention that being an entrepreneur doesn't mean you have to start your own business, you can begin to apply these methods to your every day job and you don't even need to be the boss! Start thinking like an entrepreneur and maybe you can have some of the same success. Aim to apply one of these things every day and see if you begin to see the business in a different light.

Blog 32
Marketing to a local audience

When marketing to a local audience it's all about the personal touch. Make sure you are seen in the right places, at the right time and with the right people. Often PR is a more useful tool than marketing when appealing to smaller communities...

It is important to make connections and build relationships with journalists at local publications including newspapers and glossy magazines. Ensure you know their deadlines and printing times in order to produce content at the right times. If they are given good quality content, when they need it then they are more likely to provide you with beneficial coverage, which is in effect free advertising.

Engage with the community as a whole, this could be by sponsoring a local football team or helping out a local school sports day and even litter picking. Businesses need to make sure they are giving something back to a local community and ensure they do not have a detrimental effect.

Word of mouth is extremely important within communities, with individuals talking between themselves on a daily basis. It would be a big mistake to ignore the effectiveness of word of mouth marketing and also the consequences of negative comments.

You could encourage positive word of mouth recommendations by offering a referral incentive, offer discount for people who have printed out a voucher from the website or cut it out of a local paper or for those who live within a certain radius of the business itself. Deal with negative word of mouth by engaging with the individuals, meet with them at public meetings or send a letter/email responding to their comments.

Keep up to date with local opinion and 'hot topics' by building relationships with local people, taking part in community engagement and act as a member of community yourselves. By doing this, businesses can make sure they are in the loop and not missing out on anything important. Another way to do this would be to monitor local press and follow any topics that may affect the community.

Most importantly however make sure your marketing has a local focus, focus on issues or problems that are prevalent in the community. Just like you wouldn't approach a women's magazine with a story about a new item of gym equipment for men, you wouldn't market to a local community with a campaign with no relevance. Take a moment to find the angle.

If it is a larger corporation who are looking to market on a local level it is important to ensure that the campaign remains integrated with the rest of the businesses marketing efforts and none of the elements contradict each other.

As with marketing to any market – know your audience, what they want and tell them you can provide it!

Blog 33
The Importance of Website Imagery

How would you feel if you logged onto your computer and your desktop background of your holiday from Barbados had disappeared? You were faced with a machine full of black and white text with no pictures...

Not great.

Companies have made millions of pounds creating user friendly interfaces for otherwise boring looking programmes, adding colour to blank backgrounds and comedy egg timers, all the make the experience more enjoyable for the users.

So why would companies forget these rules and create a website full of text and no images?

Imagery on websites is extremely important for two reasons.

Firstly it is essential to make your website as aesthetically appealing as it can be, if achieved you will be able to hold your visitors attention for longer and encourage them to come back. Visitors to your site don't want to be face with a screen full of text so make it interesting for them, images can break up long passages of text and can add further explanation to text. In an ideal world they should

59

complement each other, be used in conjunction to inform and entertain your reader.

The selected images need to add to the overall visual experience. Sometimes visitors can be drawn in by the use of an image which then causes them to read the text around it. However on the other extreme a website with hundreds of pictures and little text support are vague and often do not contain as much information as the visitor would like, so a good balance needs to be achieved.

Secondly, despite there being great debate, images can be used to increase optimisation of your website. Therefore images can make a difference to your ranking on Google.com. To do this however it is essential to alt tag your images, this is a 3-4 word description as to what the image is, the better the description the better results you obtain. As the famous catchphrase presenter says: Say what you see! One way to check if your description is the best it can be is to read it to a person who has not seen the image to see if they can visualise a version of the image.

Both imagery and text are important on a website and often selecting the right ones can be there hard part. You need to strike a good balance between both in order to cater to all your visitors needs and wants. One final note of warning however, it is important to remember to ensure that the images you choose are properly credited, you could open up a minefield...

Blog 34
Twitter - I'm set up, now what?

You've heard all the hype and have now taken the step and to join the social media crowd, but what next?

Before you start it is important to develop an online personality so that people know what to expect from you. If your twitter feed swaps and changes from being formal to informal followers will be confused and won't know how to engage with you as they will be unsure of how it will be met. It is essential that you ensure the personality you choose is integrated with the rest of your business and fits in with the morals and values it follows. This not only keeps communication integrated it also ensures that more than one member of staff is capable of being responsible for the companies social media. If you are an extremely corporate business such as a bank, formal and professional in style you wouldn't/shouldn't really be tweeting the same sorts of things as a business in a more informal sector as undoubtedly your target audience will differ.

The next step is to build up followers, one way to do this is to follow individuals and organisations of interest and they are likely to follow you back. Another way is to take part in tweetchats, there are lots out there, depending on your sector, so have a look! If there is, make a virtual appearance and get involved. This is one way of building followers who are relevant and who are keen to engage online.

It cannot be stressed enough to: ENGAGE, ENGAGE, ENGAGE! There is little point in joining social media if you do not engage with your followers, in fact it could be said that having a site with no movement on it for the past 5 months is worse than not having one at all. Tweet at least once a day - more if you can - reply to any messages you receive, say thank you to anyone who retweets you and make sure that you retweet any links you find interesting.

For those that claim there is not enough time in the day to do everything you need to, you're right, everyone wishes there were more hours in the day. However social media is something that is worth spending some of your time on, it gives you a chance to gather direct feedback from your customers, engage with them directly and make connections with others who could benefit your business. For those at a desk all day aim to check it 3 times a day – in the morning, at lunchtime and just before you leave – if not more.

The nature of social media means it is extremely easy to use and can be used on the go using a smart phone, meaning there isn't much of an excuse not to use it. Give social media a chance, don't just set it up and leave it, as you won't build followers and a positive online presence with no effort.

Blog 35
Why are my customers not buying?

You think you have the perfect product, customer service levels are high and sales were doing well. Your business was flourishing, but then for some reasons sales slowed and became almost stagnant. But why? You hadn't changed anything – well there you go! There lies your problem!

It is important to note that many factors could be responsible for the slowing down of sales, the recession often being one of the main causes for many businesses. Consumers are becoming increasingly skeptical and unsure about purchasing goods due to depleting amounts of disposable income and job insecurity. But slow sales aren't always to be blamed on the recession...

The market place is moving extremely fast, evolving all the time and the world is working 24 hours, 7 days a week. It is essential that your business moves with the times and doesn't get left behind.

Start by asking yourself these questions:

Is there a market for my product? For some businesses this is their first hurdle. Often entrepreneurs identify a need and seek to create a product or a service that fulfils it, however they sometimes overlook the fact that the market they are serving may not be large enough to make a sustainable business out of.

It is also important to look at your competitors. Are they taking over your market share? If so why? The technical term is competitor analysis, however put basically it is identifying your competitors and establishing what they are doing better (and worse) than you. Ensure you know what makes you different and make this your unique selling point, it is not always something to be looked upon negatively.

Are you marketing your product correctly and to the best of your ability? Are you targeting the correct people? Ensure that your customers know about your product. Even when brands and products are known about it is essential to continually market in order to remain part of the consumers' repertoire of brands.

For example, Coca Cola is known worldwide and is one of the largest, most successful manufacturers of soft drinks, but they still advertise. Why? Because they want to achieve top of the mind awareness, in a perfect Coca Cola world: Consumer thinks 'I'm thirsty' and instantly associates the feeling with how refreshed they would feel after a drink of Coca Cola.

A consumers repertoire of brands shifts and changes for many reasons, some of which are known about such as reference groups, self concepts, how the product solves their problem and others which have no explanation. That is until market researchers are able to mind read...(Say hello to neuromarketing...)

Marketing communications has 4 main functions, it aims to:

    Differentiate
    Remind
    Inform
    Persuade

So give your business a chance and make sure that you: differentiate yourself from competitors, remind consumers of exactly who you are and what you do, inform them of what you can offer and persuade them your company is the one for them!

Blog 36
Top tips for Social Media engagement

Now that your company has a Twitter/ Facebook/ Flickr/ LinkedIn/ Behance account it is time to engage! Easier said than done, well not really, just remember to be SOCIAL...

S**PAM – don't do it!**

Give followers what they want, if and when they want it. If they haven't expressed an interest then don't bombard them with endless messages full of self promotion and 'exclusive' offers. Engagement is a two-way communication process, if you aren't receiving any feedback then that's not engagement – that's promotion. And trust me, people will get sick of it and are more than likely to 'defriend' you.

O**pinions**

By all means, give your opinions but stay out of the 'how not to do it' gang. It is so easy to get carried away and make your opinion know but remember on the internet the information is accessible to everyone and often misdemeanors spread faster than wildfire – so a word of warning. Understand that everything you do will be open to misinterpretation and even if you notice your error and delete the comment, it is still possible that someone took a screen shot and you could end up in hot water.

Choose a brand personality

And stick to it! Ensure that the personality that your company projects online is consistent and fits in with the overall brand values. If you are a fun, lively office make sure that you project that. Social media offers a brilliant way for customers and other individuals to become involved with the business and feel part of your business. If they build up a relationship with the company they are more likely to remain loyal as they will feel an 'emotional' connection to it, often a powerful differentiating factor.

Interest

Be interesting. People don't engage with boring brands, so post fun links, make jokes and use 'hot topics' as a basis of your comments. By keeping up to date with what is happening to your customers then you can make sure what you are saying is relevant and people are more likely to respond if it something they have an opinion on. Take note of a previous point, be careful making comments on very controversial topics as you suffer negative repercussions.

Answer

Everyone Say a quick thank you or tell them to have a nice day, even if someone retweets a link make sure that you tweet them back to express your gratitude and they will be likely to do it again. Respond to questions, links, retweets and messages. By being friendly and accessible your company reputation will only benefit. The nature of social media means that responses can be sent quickly and from almost anywhere so there is no excuse.

Look around

Check out your Klout score, keep track of the number of Twitter followers, measure your reach, see where your followers are coming from. There are hundreds of measurement tools out there for you to measure your effectiveness online so use them! You wouldn't enter into any other type of communication with consumers without being able to measure its effectiveness and social media isn't any different. Online advertising click through rates can be measured and you can even track an individual's click process to see where they travelled from and to.

When used correctly social media is an extremely powerful tool, it is a fantastic way to engage with consumers in a fast and convenient way. It allows consumers to get closer to the organisation and get a real feel for the company, be aware of this and harness the positives, however ensure that you acknowledge the negatives and don't become a case study online of a company who has used it inappropriately...

Blog 37
Website design - Where do I start?

It can be a scary prospect creating the first website for your business, even if your business has just begun or if your business is already established making the technological move to have your own website can be daunting, but as you might have guessed essential.

The majority of businesses are at least listed on Google places even if they don't have their own website so securing your own domain is a logical and valuable asset to have. Individuals are using the internet for even the simplest of tasks and are more likely to research their options online before heading to the high street. Therefore having a website could make the difference between a consumer choosing between you and a competitor.

A small price to pay when it could mean the difference between survival or bankruptcy.

You could brave it alone, head out into the vast arena of the internet and build your own website using Wordpress.com, buildyourownsite.co.uk or one of the other sites available. If you are technologically minded or have a friend who is willing to help out this might be a viable option, especially if funds are extremely tight.

However web designers aren't as expensive as first thought and the service you receive will make your website stand out from those that have been built by an unprofessional individual. You will be guided through the process from start to finish and you can be as hands on, or hands off if the case may be, as you like. If you build up a good relationship with your designer you will be able to develop your vision together safe in the knowledge that they know what they are doing.

When thinking of setting up your new website, whether that be alone or with the help of a designer, think about:

- The 'feel' of the site – what do you want to project? A professional image? Corporate or fun?
- Information to be contained – what will the website be used for? Purchasing goods? Finding out information?
- What sections do you want on the website?
- What will your website be called? Is that domain available?
- Is your current logo suitable? Can it be used online?
- Will you be using any other social media sites?
- Research similar sites and see what they have done – will yours be similar or completely different? You could build up a mood board of the type of thing you would like and maybe ones that you don't.

- Get quotes from different website designers; ask your friends or business colleagues for recommendations. Word of mouth recommendations are the best way to recruit website designers as if someone has experienced their work then that's the best advertisement they could have.

Blog 38
What does a marketing plan involve?!

The importance of having a well crafted marketing plan is stressed again and again but what is it and what does it involve? Does it include adverts? What about customers? Is it my product? How do I know when I have finished?

Firstly it is important to note that different businesses will place emphasis on different parts of the marketing plan and might not include all the points mentioned. However the 10 main factors listed should at least be considered when approaching your marketing plan:

1. Background analysis

   Whether you use PEST (political, economic, social, technological) or SWOT (strengths, weaknesses, opportunities, threats) or even PRESTCOM…don't ask…there are thousands of variations that businesses use to remind themselves the factors to think about when analysing the business environment. If abbreviations aren't your thing just remember: to look at what affects your business both internally and externally.

2. Marketing objectives

   What exactly do you want to do? Do you want to get consumers to go to a website? Feel an emotion or think differently about your product/service? Don't embark on a campaign before you know what you want to do – it is almost like setting off on a long journey without knowing where you are going, you will never know when you have got there or whether you are going in the right direction! Pointless...and not fun when it costs money.

3. Budget

It's usually a good job if you check whether you can afford what you are setting out to do. Otherwise go back to level 2 and reassess. Different companies have different methods of setting their budget, all have their advantages and disadvantages. It is a good idea to find one that works of everyone in your organisation, however acknowledge the limitations of certain methods. One to definitely avoid in my opinion is matching the competition, this is unmarked territory, you never know their full situation and they may well have financial backing from somewhere else. One of the best methods is 'objective and task', pick your objective and find out how much it will cost, then check if you can afford. That way you have the best chance of achieving the set objectives because you have sufficient resources.

4. Target market/audience

Your target market is who the product is designed for, the user. The target audience is who you are aiming your marketing communications at, other members of the decision making process, they might not be users of the product but they might have purchasing power. It is important you make this distinction and alter your message and media accordingly.

5. Set communications objectives and message

Decide exactly what you want to say to the identified audience. Make sure it fits in with in them and will help you achieve your overall marketing objective.

6. Strategy

    Where will you focus your efforts? You could push your product through the system by convincing wholesalers or retailers to stock your product or, you could pull it through by advertising to consumers and getting them to hassle retailers to stock your product. However focusing on just one strategy can be risky, especially for new products, as there is no point having a retailer stocking your product if no-one wants to purchase it.

7. Develop campaign

    Now is your time to choose how you get your message across. Get into the minds of your target audience and focus your efforts where you think they are likely to see your message and acknowledge it. In other words don't focus on building a strong social media presence when your target audience is aged 80+ and they don't use the internet. Different methods are better suited to certain tasks so use your knowledge of the different methods, strengths and weaknesses to make the most of the tools available to you.

8. Test the mix

    This stage can be approached with varying degrees of formality. If there was an endless budget and no timescale then in-depth market research would be useful to see how consumers would respond to the communications tools of your campaign however this is not always an option. Other methods to test your communications mix include informal focus groups, asking friends and family for objective feedback or even placing yourself in customers shoes.

9. Co-ordination and integration

    Some businesses contract out some of the work to agencies whilst others keep it all in house, some make the use of both. However no matter how your campaign is run it needs to remain integrated and cohesive so check how it is being co-ordinated. Have regular meetings and keep on top of all the big decisions.

10. Monitor and Evaluation

How do you know if you have been successful? Go back to step 2 and 5 and place a big tick by the side of them if you have indeed achieved what you set out to. You have permission to pat yourself on the back too. If you haven't then look back and see what you could do differently.

That's it, your marketing plan. There is of course more involved, this is a blueprint, however if you use this as your basis and adapt it for your individual business then you won't miss out anything important.

Blog 39
What is the shelf life of a company website?

To put it bluntly: it depends!

For many companies their website acts as the face of the organisation, a perfectly built website full of relevant, up to date information for customers and the media. However other companies have let their websites slip, when they were first launched their websites were everything they could have wanted and more, but times have changed and so have needs and wants. Whilst this is the cheapest option it is a dangerous tactic as you run the risk of looking outdated and your website putting customers off rather than enticing them.

With increasing numbers of companies joining the market place in all sectors it is difficult to shine out through all the noise created by your competitors – what better way than with a well crafted and professional website? Don't get left behind, guaranteed your competitors won't be missing this trick...

Content itself is subject to change. Staff may get new Twitter accounts and phone numbers may change therefore it is essential to keep these details up to date. Also when consumers / potential suppliers or the media access your website they are keen to see new content including client case studies and new pictures. One way to ensure an area of your website is constantly updated is to include a Twitterfeed, therefore every time you tweet it will appear on the site. By providing new content, visitors to the site are more likely to come back to check for new information and see you as a credible source.

As well as the content the design of the website itself is important, as everyone knows fashions change and websites are the same. Depending on the design you choose it might quickly go out of fashion or it might remain timeless and just require little tweaks. Either way you will need to assess your website periodically and ask yourself if it is giving the best impression of your business that it can. Remember to keep your website integrated with other elements of your business and ensure that logos, fonts and pictures are used across all mediums. It is useful to build up good relationship with your website designer to create a design that you are happy with and that matches your business personality.

When it is so easy to keep websites up to date and designs fresh and professional don't let the face of the organisation slip. The cost to your reputation could be deadly.

Blog 40
Dangers of social networking

Often people focus on the benefits of something and ignore the dangers they bring until they come back to bite you on the bottom, consequently you often have to learn the hard way.

As with anything with the benefits come dangers, however by knowing these dangers in advance and learning from others mistakes you are less likely to be caught out.

1. SPAM

Threat: By opening a Facebook page and allowing users to upload their own content you could become the victim of SPAM by users uploading irrelevant content onto your site in order to get it noticed.

Fix: All social networking sites offer the choice to delete certain content so as long as the site is checked on a daily basis (at least) then inappropriate content won't stay there for long.

2. Untrue reviews

Threat: Competitors uploading fake reviews of your products and making false allegations against your company.

Fix: Be wary of this. As with any complaint take seriously and respond. However if it is found to be a competitor there are legal routes that you could pursue.

3. Bad news travels fast

Threat: So your organisation hasn't done something particularly well, you might have made a mistake. However with the rise of the 24/7 society this news will travel extremely fast and there are limited ways as to how you can prevent it from doing so. Instead of customers sharing their experiences with their friends they can now share it on a worldwide stage.

Fix: Put out a response and make sure that it spreads just as fast and far as the mistake did. Use the tools to your advantage, the fact that news can travel so quickly is not a bad thing when it is information you want to share. Respond to complaints and try to rectify the problem with customers – the move towards relationship marketing has been emphasised by this trend, so embrace it!

4. Employees talking about the organisation online

Threat: There is the possibility that employees might go home and moan what a horrible day they have had at work on their Facebook wall, this is something that used to happen anyway but the implications are more serious than if they were to just talk to their friends about it at the pub.

Fix: Draw up a policy and warn employees of the consequences of talking about the company online. Make it clear from the beginning of what will happen. Prevent the situation from happening.

Blog 41
How to collect an email base

We have already established that in some situations email shots are an effective way to communicate with consumers. Quick and cost effective they offer a modern alternative to mail shots. All well and good, but how do you build a collection of people to send them to?

It is important to point out that there are some 'businesses' who choose to do things below board, they purchase lists of email address from fellow dishonest 'businesses'. This is not an option, it reflects badly on the organisation and opens a data confidentiality minefield so is best avoided at all costs. However here are some better options to help build your email base:

Give an option in store

If your customers are in store they are likely to be interested in information about special deals or sales you may be holding, so harness this interest and teach staff to give them the option to opt into subscribing for the e-shots whilst they are purchasing their goods.

Have the option to sign up on the website

Harnessing a customer's interest doesn't just have to be in store, it can be at any other critical control point they have with your business, whether they phone up, see it on the bottom of their receipt or log onto the website. Give them the option! When they register for the website there could be a simple tick box that asks them if they want to sign up or automatically signs them up unless they click the opt out box.

Offer clear incentives

Customers are more likely to agree to sign up to something if they are clear of the reasons why they should and what benefits they are likely to receive. So tell them! Have a sample e-shot on the website so they can view it and decide if it is something they might be interested in, assure them that they will receive news about sales and special discounts before others.

Recommend to others

Do not underestimate the power of word of mouth. Offer customers an incentive if they recommend others to your email base, sharing information has been made easier by the use of the internet so use this to your advantage. It takes on average around 10 seconds to forward an email, encourage customers to do this and it could mean a lot more business for you.

Buddy up!

This is where environmental scanning is important, if you can find an existing newsletter that caters to the same/similar target market as yourself then ask them if they can promote your newsletter by mentioning it at the bottom of their own. Obviously your competitor is not likely to do this, if they do, then well done you! However you are more likely to get a complementary company to do it. For example, if you sell television stands then television manufacturers who don't manufacture their own stands would be classed as a complementary company.

Please note, it is important to provide an 'opt out' option and you MUST abide by it, if a customer does not want to receive your newsletter they should have the option to opt out made available to them and it must be easy to do.

Blog 42
What are royalty free images?

We've already established that the use of images on websites is extremely important when trying to engage visitors' attention and to increase the aesthetic appeal of the site.

Sometimes referred to as RF images, royalty free images can be used for commercial uses by businesses. By paying a one-off fee, contracts then determine whether the image can be used a fixed number of times or give you unlimited use and there is no need to purchase additional licenses.

Unless you deal with images on a regular basis then the different licenses needed to use an image can seem like an endless battle with minefields blocking your path on either side, royalty free images take away these dangers. Once you have paid your initial fee you don't need to worry about getting into any trouble with licensing as it will be done and dusted.

Another advantage of the one off fee means that you can keep on top of your finances and understand exactly when and where your money is going and what it is for. It is important to note that the images are available relatively cheaply and can be downloaded as soon as they are needed meaning if you are on a tight budget and time constrained they may be the best option.

So you've decided that you want to use royalty free images – but where do you get them? There are thousands of websites offering images and sometimes specific artists, photographers and designers are offering their own. Have a look around and find the best ones for you and your business.

However a lot of the images on these websites are quite generic, so if your business has a particular vision or would like something specific then it might be a better idea to employ a photographer who you can talk through your ideas with and get the exact image you would like.

Also royalty free images are available for everyone to use. There is nothing to stop your competitors from using the same, this could confuse customers and mean that the time and money you have invested into building your reputation could be worthless if consumers become confused.

If used in the correct situation and acknowledge the limitations disadvantages then royalty free images can offer a great alternative to employing a photographer to create an image.

Blog 43
What should an e-shot include?

Firstly it would be helpful to start with what an e-shot actually is.

And no, they are not as scary as they sound!

E-shots are targeted emails which are sent to existing and potential customers via email. They have two main purposes, one of which is marketing. They are a fantastic way of alerting people to your products and services efficiently and they are an alternative to some marketing tools such as leaflets. They can also be used to maintain customer retention levels, by reminding customers of your existence and you can ensure you are the place they come to when they want to make a repeat or similar purchase – you achieve top of the mind awareness which is valuable in achieving customer loyalty.

E-shots can contain links, images and text so are a great tool when wanting convey a variety of content. Information contained in the email should be relevant to the consumer or it may well become mixed up with SPAM. SPAM is a dreaded word to marketers, some individuals define SPAM as any irrelevant information that they receive. A company that is associated with sending SPAM is in danger of bringing their reputation down and sometimes it can destroy the image that your brand has worked hard in achieving. However this can be avoided by making sure you have the recipient's permission to be sending them an e-shot and ensuring that the information contained is of interest.

It is a good idea to have links to articles on your website in order to direct traffic to your website and encourage customers to look around. This could be done by including a link to the 'product/service of the month' or the one with the biggest discount available to the most popular. Once a customer is on your website they are more likely to look around and see what else you have available, plus it might just prompt them to order what they have needed.

Customers like to feel special and rewarding their loyalty can encourage them to remain so. One way to do this could be by using e-shots to communicate information to them before it goes live on the website. By making the recipients of your e-shots feel as if they are receiving benefits by subscribing to your e-shots they are more likely to remain subscribed and recommend your shots to friends.

Blog 44
Words of warning – email marketing

Whilst sending out interesting and permission based e-shots is an effective way of engaging with your customers and enticing potential customers when done wrong they can cause a lot of damage to your brands reputation. But by following these handy hints your company reputation will stay intact and your e-shots will be useful to customers:

Don't send out your e-shots too often

See 'How often should I be sending my e-shots?' (Blog 30) for a few pointers.

Be wary of personalisation

Personalisation is a great tool when used effectively but used incorrectly it can make your e-shots look unprofessional and reminiscent of SPAM. Ask the customer themselves how they would like to be addressed on the registration form and stick to it. Ensure that it has replaced the text properly and no mistakes have been made.

Offer the 'opt out' option

And stick to it. It is essential to make it easy for e-shot recipients to opt out of receiving the emails and it is equally important to stick to your word. Therefore if someone requests to be taken from your distribution list ensure this is done quickly and they no longer receive anything. If not this could reflect badly on your business and they could see you as a nuisance.

Ensure all the links work and correspond with the correct part of the website

You have done the hard part of building your distribution list, your recipient has opened the email but the link in the e-shot doesn't work...you've just lost a visitor to your website...so a lot of your efforts were wasted. It is easy to check if the links work properly so do it!

Ensure that your e-shots are integrated with the rest of the business

It is extremely important to ensure that all your marketing communications tools are integrated to ensure that your customers don't become confused by different styles and tones. This applies to your e-shots. They should include the same font as the website and carry the company logo. The content itself should be written in the same style as all the other literature such as that included on the website and any leaflets.

Blog 45
What social media icons should I include?

The world of social media is vast and the number of social media platforms is increasingly on a daily basis. With thousands of sites out there how do you know which icons to offer your visitors?

It is essential to make it easy for visitors to share links to your site, the easier it is, the more likely users are to do it. By sharing links, visitors are encouraging others to visit your site and are effectively giving it their seal of approval. Sharing links online could be likened to 'online word of mouth'.

So how do you decide? The simple answer to this question would be to say: provide all of them!

However, in reality this would make your website full of unused social media icons and the probability of all them being used is highly unlikely. Not only this, but the aesthetic appeal of your site would also be affected.

One of the best ways to decide is to keep up to date with the social media platforms that are popular at the time and check out infographics to see the platforms your target audience are using. Start with the basic and most popular social media icons and you can always add more at a later date.

Another way is to ask your target audience what icons they would like included. By engaging with your target audience directly you will find out exactly what they are using, plus this would offer an opportunity for you to carry out some informal market research as you could ask them what they like and don't like about your site and make changes accordingly. By building a relationship with your audience it makes it possible to find out about any trends that are occurring and ensure that you keep on top of them.

The mains icons to ensure that you include are: Facebook, Twitter, Google Bookmarks, Google Buzz, Del.icio.us, Digg, StumbleUpon and Reddit.

However new platforms are emerging on a daily basis so keep your eyes peeled for the latest social media tools and websites!

Blog 46
Top 3 upcoming social media sites

It is extremely difficult to make predictions about the future of social media due to the nature of social media itself – however the trends that are popular and those that seem to be emerging are:

1. Quora

    Quora is effectively a question and answer site. It allows users to ask a question and to receive answers, they are answered by the users of the site themselves and then Quora produces an amalgamation of all the answers. It is reminiscent of Wikipedia however it doesn't strive for objectivity as anyone is allowed to answer with their subjective opinion.

2. Klout

    We all like to know how well we are doing and see how we compare to others. This is exactly what Klout offers, it allows you to measure your online influence against others. The higher your score to 100 the more influential you are! It also allows you to see who the most influential people are online.

3. Diaspora

   Could this be the new Facebook? According to the content on the site it claims you can share what you want with who you want. It is said to have more privacy settings than Facebook and with recent debate about the privacy settings on Facebook it could offer a great alternative.

There is no doubt that there will be some great advancement within social networking in 2014, so keep your eye on these sites and any others that may arise.

Blog 47
How do people know you have a website?

You've set up your business and decided to have a website – brilliant idea! What better way to raise awareness and educate people as to what you can offer. But how do you direct traffic to your site? How do your existing customers or potential customers even know it exists?

SEO

When you are looking for a company to carry out a task where is one of the first places that you go? You type it into a search engine on the internet. In most households the internet has taken over from the phonebook as users are able to type in a name or a service and thousands of providers appear. By using various tips to increase your SEO you will appear higher on the search results and are therefore more likely to be the lucky link to be clicked. By appearing high in the search engine rankings visitors assume you are professional and are at the top of your trade giving the impression that you can be trusted. Research it for yourself or speak to an individual who specialises in SEO.

Other marketing communication tools

Make the most of the other tools at your disposal. For example, if you send out an e-shot ensure you put links to your website on them to direct traffic towards the site. Or if you have done mail shots, ensure you include the website address to inform people that you have a website. Print it on the bottom of the receipt, tell customers about it in store, over the phone or on their invoices. By informing people that you have launched a website they are more likely to check it out. If they don't know it exists then they might not look for it!

Social media

This is a brilliant way of directing traffic to your website. You could tweet links to your followers or share links on Facebook to certain articles on your site and encourage others to share links. Social media is a great way to build up a buzz around the launch of your site, one option is to have a countdown. Tell your followers that you are launching a new site and keep them up to date with progress. By initiating this excitement about the new site customers are more likely to visit the site to see the changes that have taken place.

Advertise

Another way to direct traffic to your website is to advertise online, by doing this it enables visitors to click directly through to your website from the advertisement.

It is important to note that the methods outlined above are effective individually but are even more effective when used in conjunction with each other. By using all the methods together you will ensure that visitors know your website exist and that they are able to access it easily. Don't let all your efforts on building a fantastic website go to waste.

Blog 48
How does Apple market so effectively?

Apple are market leaders.

They create the need, by telling consumers what they want and what they need, they then proceed to fulfil this need with their shiny new products with touch screens and gyroscopes (the gizmo in the IPhone 4 that makes the screen revolve.)

But how do they do it?

Unfortunately there is no definitive answer and if anyone did find out the secret ingredient the possibility of it being printed in a book is unlikely to say the least.

However there are some main trends which could be responsible for the success of Apples' marketing communications:

They are risk takers.

Steve Jobs, former Chief Executive of Apple famously said that Apple carry out no market research, for most businesses this is an extremely risky tactic but it has certainly paid off for Apple. Instead of following trends, they are at the forefront and leading at an incredible pace. There is no guarantee that the market for their product exists but they plough on regardless and the release of their products cause some of the largest queues known to man. It is important to note however that they don't enter into decisions to take a product to launch blindly as they invest millions into the innovation of new products.

They are good at being talked about.

Apple are the masters of creating a buzz. They are extremely innovative and understand that the release of new products with new features means PR opportunities – rumours of what features the new product contains, reviews by prominent and influential bloggers. Their reputation precedes them, because they are interesting, people talk about them and quite rightly so.

They understand personalisation.

Apple realise that consumers like to make things their own and until recently all technology has looked the same however by offering consumers a choice of colour of their 'idevices' it allows consumers to feel as if they are expressing themselves. There are also skins available to personalise your ipod, iPhone or ipad even more.

They have fans.

Apple are a fantastic example of a brand with a high level of brand loyalty. For example consumers in the market for a mobile telephone have two main choices when choosing a smart phone: iPhone or Android, often consumers feel very strongly about their choice. Apple has strong brand loyalists who act as advocates and recommend the brand to others, almost like recruiting members to the gang.

They have integrated marketing communications.

Their marketing communications are all carefully integrated so consumers know what to expect and can recognise an Apple advert straight away due to their distinctive style. Their adverts focus on the product, are simple and showcase the product.

Apple just seem to have everything right, all the elements of a successful business just link in and create what is: Apple. Keep an eye out for what they do next!

Blog 49
Where do businesses miss a marketing trick?

Some businesses believe that marketing is the production of leaflets or broadcasting an advert, however, this is only half the battle. The definition of marketing itself can make the difference as to where companies miss out, for example if a company believes marketing is used purely for recruiting new customers then they will miss out on customer retention strategies.

There are some common marketing mistakes:

1. **Not marketing their company at all due to the preconception that it is too expensive.**

   Contrary to belief, marketing does not have to swallow up all your profits, admittedly however, some marketing communication tools are more expensive than others. If you are a small business, then nationwide television advertising might not be within your budget, however this doesn't mean you can't afford to do any marketing for your business. You could concentrate on making the most of PR opportunities or place an advert in the local paper. Marketing doesn't have to cost the world, you just have to be creative.

2. **Not knowing your target audience.**

   If you don't know who you are aiming your marketing communications at, then how are you going to do it effectively? Underestimating the need to understand your customers can be fatal to a business as after all, if your customers don't buy your product or use your service then your company is not likely to exist. The marketing concept argues that organisations 'should satisfy consumers needs and wants to make profits' to do this companies should stay close to consumers, however in order to get close to customers you need to know who they are!

3. **Marketing in the wrong places.**

    This point follows on from above, if you don't know who your target audience are then how are you going to reach them? It is possible for a company to spend the majority of their marketing budget, which let's be blunt, is often a struggle to obtain, by concentrating efforts in the wrong places. For example, if your aim is to target 14 year old girls then it seems obvious that you wouldn't advertise in Men's Health magazine. So place yourself in the shoes of the target audience and think about the type of media you would access, and the types you wouldn't.

4. **The non-existent marketing objective.**

    Marketing is a journey and it is extremely rare that you ever set off on a journey with no idea where your final destination may be, so why do the same with your marketing? Without clear marketing objectives it is impossible to know whether you have achieved what you set out to do, so when asked the question: what's the point? You would be unable to answer. Set clear objectives and evaluate your progress regularly, this will ensure your efforts will be worthwhile and your results are tangible.

5. **Not integrating marketing communications.**

    Inconsistencies do nothing but confuse customers and give the impression that the company is disjointed and unorganised. If Coca Cola can manage a worldwide image and ensure all their marketing communications are integrated then why can't your business? Simple points such as ensuring your logo is consistent, typeface is the same and the same tone is kept throughout channels are good starting points. Customers like to know what to expect from businesses and are more likely to stay loyal to companies who they trust and recognise.

Blog 50
Top 5 functions every website should have

A website is a fantastic way of conveying tailored information about what your business is about and services it can offer.

However there are certain functions that visitors look for on each page that they visit. If you acknowledge these functions and ensure that your website caters for these requirements then you will have a website that is a pleasure for users to visit.

Websites should...

...be easy to navigate

Information should be clearly laid out and visitors should be able to navigate their way around easily.

...contain clear and up to date content

There is nothing worse than logging onto a website that contains out of date and incorrect information about an organisation. The beauty of websites means that they can be changed easily and the changes take place immediately. So there is no excuse!

...provide contact information

Not only this, but they should contain clear information on job roles and responsibilities, websites should also provide telephone numbers and email addresses for staff members. If your organisation decides to have a 'contact us' pages which encourages visitors to enter their details for you to get in touch then ensure that their requests are dealt with efficiently and quickly.

...enable visitors to search the site itself

By offering a site search to visitors it enables them to search the site itself to easily find the information they need. It is important to note however that the results of the site search need to be relevant and presented in a simple way so that they don't confuse visitors more.

...be quick to load

A websites welcoming page shouldn't be overloaded with information so that it takes a long time to load. Visitors are likely to get bored and frustrated with the page and are likely to click off and try again later or go elsewhere.

When designing your website think about your personal experiences of using websites, think about the functions that you like using on websites and try to include them on your own site. Make using your website satisfying and easy to use and your visitors are more likely to come back...

Notes

Notes

Notes

Notes

Out Soon….

Social Media

50 useful blog articles to help create a buzz online.

www.ingramcontent.com/pod-product-compliance
Lightning Source LLC
Chambersburg PA
CBHW061515180526
45171CB00001B/183